Little Hunger

Little Hunger

POEMS

Philip Kevin Paul

NIGHTWOOD EDITIONS

Nightwood Editions
P.O. Box 1779
Gibsons, BC V0N 1V0
Canada
www.nightwoodeditions.com

Cover art by Chris Paul (www.chrispaul.ca)
Printed and bound in Canada

Nightwood Editions acknowledges financial support from the
Government of Canada through the Book Publishing Industry
Development Program and the Canada Council for the Arts,
and from the Province of British Columbia through the British
Columbia Arts Council and the Book Publisher's Tax Credit.

THE CANADA COUNCIL | LE CONSEIL DES ARTS
FOR THE ARTS | DU CANADA
SINCE 1957 | DEPUIS 1957

BRITISH
COLUMBIA
ARTS COUNCIL
Supported by the Province of British Columbia

Library and Archives Canada Cataloguing in Publication

Paul, Philip Kevin, 1971–
    Little hunger / Philip Kevin Paul.

Poems.
ISBN 978-0-88971-220-1

    I. Title.

PS8581.A8295L58 2008   C811'.6   C2008-905869-0

For Tanya
My dreamings wouldn't be as sweet.
STWIEⱠ TƑE NE S'HELI EꞀ NE₵E

Contents

iii.

I.

When the Stones Cleared Their Throats to Sing

This morning the water was clear,
dear diary, high ebb, but a summer
depth of shoreline, nearly enough
warm gravel for my mother's family
to all gather in one place.

Just as my father never got
used to his false teeth,
the ocean jerks stones
carried from elsewhere
in the winter storms. I'm alone
for my morning bath —
first time I have to say prayers
in **SENĆOŦEN** without Uncle.

Under water the stones sound
as if they're stuttering mid-vowel...

Okay, stones,
tell me about the journey,
about what you lost
to turn so round
you look soft.
And kingfisher, raven, juniper:
None of you interrupt.

On Their Wedding Anniversary

The father I remember strode from one to the other
of our stolen islands. In a fit of rage he tore out
our most rugged trees as he walked, then sat down
on a low mountain, throat swollen with apologies
he couldn't give. Still the people praised him.
That made him sad. It disappointed him.
Baffled by his inability to cry, he stroked the trees
along the flat of the mountaintop like soft hair
on the dog he went seeking loneliness with.

The son I was then withdrew, silenced
by the stranger my father had become.
Silence is all a son has for such distance.
For rage, the son offers a cast-down look;
for disappointment, chores done quietly before dawn.

And my mother? She waited for the peace
she knew was coming. She waited for a love
she knew would rise in her husband
and be enough. She waited for a time he would go
all the way into the true heart of his territory,
and come all the way back home. She waited
at the doorway of their fine language.

In answer to this waiting, her delight
made me what I'd always tried to be
when she praised the four new buds
on the apple tree we thought long dead.

But in the east, south, west, north
walls of the rain, she didn't have to wait.
Her arm around my waist, my arm
slung over her shoulder, we stood
in the best east-facing window.

This was *our* place, inside false dawn's rain.

And here is the son I've become. I write
the names of the secret on all my mirrors
until I'm standing where love has been
chased so deep it has become sorrow.
Only here do I know, like my mother,
the sound of the earth's drinking
is water clacking steadily from a gutter
in need of repair or cleaning; the slop
of fat rain falling into a wheelbarrow
full of rain; the sound of her flat-footed son
running barefoot up the wet driveway
to get the newspaper.

It was the best of hungers
that sent me looking on a day like this—
the rain pulling something up
with its unbreakable strands
and putting down
what it will return to collect later.

Out of Place

I.
As the story goes,
Dad called the pigeon over
and it hopped weakly
into his palm and rested
its head on his wrist—
an albino pigeon, outcast,
living breath by breath.
No surprise, no amusement
between my mother and father
when the bird obeyed.

Dad got to business,
pinching at its breastbone.
The tired, ugly bird dozed
in the crook of his arm.
It had no answer for
the rude attention of children
pulling open its eyelids
to see its red pupils.

Nursed to health by a man
who seemed too big for the job,
through spring and summer
we watched it become human.
It slept on the corner of Dad's
pillow, ate from a bowl
at the breakfast table,
preferred warm water when

it bathed in the kitchen sink.
How proud it looked
while Dad made fat rolling
waves in the garden, readying
the soil for early seed.

II.

The summer I was nine years old, I got my father
to myself just once: a luckless day of fishing,
and when we turned toward home we did
what all bad fishermen do and continued
trolling into the bay, past all the best spots.
Mid-bay the rod quivered feebly. Dad said
it must be an ill thing, far in and living up shallow.

Sure enough, it didn't fight much, so I got to
reel it all the way in. It rolled over—how sadly,
and never jumped. When it surfaced I looked
to Dad for explanation, but he also needed
someone to look to. When he cut the outboard,
both of us were shut inside a silence—
barely enough room for a child and his father.
It was an albino salmon, white as milk,
eyes shining like droplets of water
sitting in a hard red leaf. The lunch cooler emptied
for saltwater, Dad put the fish in and worked
the hook, stirring it clockwise, then counter—
so calmly he became someone I didn't come from.

The hook out, we turned back toward the point
and deeper water, the cooler sturdied
on my lap. I drummed gently on its side
and Dad sang a familiar serenity back into the day.
He lowered the salmon into the water as I've seen
mothers lower a sleeping child into a father's
arms. The salmon didn't lose one drop of blood.
I thought the whiter a thing, the less blood it had.

III.

Dad's gone. Ten years he's had no name.
The headstones, bleached and well kept,
are the only white things in this graveyard.
The rotting fence shows what tree it was,
and nearly in the centre, a statue of Mary
is tarnished black. Pigeons have woven
a veil for her that no one notices —
thankless work. That's my dad talking,
still talking in and through me:

Stupid woman, he might say.
She is facing exactly the wrong direction
to be standing among our dead.

IV.

The trees have forked false dawn
with their branches.
How long my eyes
have been turned down,

working memory out
of its natural vagueness.
Getting its way,
memory would have me
making greater heroes of the dead,
and greater loss.

How close Dad lived
to what he couldn't know:
the albino pigeon, an unwanted bird.
The albino salmon we watched
until it went too deep for us to see
— its last white flicker
was what we held in other darknesses;
and "Backwards Mary," intruder and gift,
scrubbed by those old enough to be sure
about what did and didn't belong,
and what needed to be done.

From the shore the old sang for the young
who paddled out keeping Mary
faced in the right direction for burial—
then tipped face-first off the planks
where she'd stood between two canoes.

Someone would remark later
that she had turned slowly in thanks,
looking back at the young men
and the last light.

Still a World for Such?

> Told not to be afraid
> of what good eyes can see,
> the young man learned not to be afraid.
> But childhood is not made
> warned against taking things for granted —
> such as Uncle and his heron wing
> brushing all who entered
> his little house, routinely asking,
> "What have you seen this week?"

There were years and years:
public school, college, university,
when the young man practised
pushing further and further inward
what had been given him
and no longer seemed of use.
Superstition.

Sitting with a girl he was too fond of,
an eight-foot heron crane bowed behind her.
He missed most of what she was saying,
not because he could hear the crane calling.
It was his silence he was ashamed of —
the rattle of excuses for putting off
the choice to live away from the laws of one world,
far back
    somewhere,
    sounding
beautiful as crane-song across distances.

What is the life you feel?
This can be taught.

Good eyes are from another dreaming.
This can be taught.

A young man walks away
toward smaller risks
in the company of a girl
he is too fond of.

And there are fewer and fewer
who know what good eyes can see,
fewer who visit with the dead
while a cold blooms inside,
few who have shivered while listening
with one ear, say, for the telephone
or a late-night walker, the other ear
to an uncle who rarely visited
in his eighty-eight years.

He asks what the young man has seen this week
and talks again about the heron wing
he found on the side of the road,
the road he walked every day through dawn
thirteen miles to shovel coal.

Song for the Place of Deer

A man and his nephew are perched high on a mountain ledge above a young forest. The trees are young because the old ones burned down in an era of war. The story lives in both nephew and uncle. When they speak about Saanich they mean the best and most ancient parts they dream of themselves.

The uncle has the rough hands of hard labour. When he rubs them together they make the sound of pea sand heaved by a long-breathed tide. He laughs a little about growing old.

He coughs, chuckles, says to the mountain, "I'm growing old," still catching his breath after the climb. The nephew, imagining the weight of what his uncle carries, and hoping to place his mind under some of it, takes the lead, telling a story about being chased down by a deer.

"I'm ready to take it back now," the uncle says before the nephew is finished his story, meaning the lead but especially what he considers his obligation. ONEST TONES, the uncle says—Saanich words, bare as the ocean shining behind the young trees' heads.

So the uncle leads and the nephew joins, better these years at making no seam when entering into song, exhaling song at the precise verse his uncle has come to: a song for the young and old trees alike, the song that remembers a simpler war that set the old world ablaze.

Descent Into Saanich

I.

A little past midnight, Saanich is scarred with light.
Over our islands, both darknesses pervade.
I know by heart the sound I can't hear
the water making as it slides against
the east end of our smallest islands
and then closes along the west shore.
The sound lays claim to me, a child of Saanich.
From under the tongue, someone teaches me.

One scar of light made into two:
the one I judged from the distance;
and the one guiding us in — I'm glad for it now
that we're close to touching down.

II.

The mornings are dark well into the steady whir
of traffic — sad machines carrying people,
many who stopped going anywhere long ago.

Slanted homeward, you realize
you can no longer go home. But don't worry,
this is the best of your longing so far.

It's Already Here

It'll come, Grandma says
my growing despair
over joblessness
and the swell of silences
between my brothers and me.
I can't see my role in it all,
I say, near tears. *It will come,*
it will come, she says.

Some of us were made from
a simple wooden spindle:
a disk with a hole in it,
and a wooden staff
tapered at both ends
and fat in the middle
so it couldn't drop
through the hole.

The road rises and rises away
from her place to mine.
When she could still walk
the path down to her beach—
I must've been very young—
she asked the sunset and me,
dusk herding the light quietly down,

Can you imagine how small
a hummingbird's egg must be?

Doorways to a Younger World

Nephew dropped carrot, corn and pole-bean seed into my ear
while I slept. When I woke he told me so, smiling into a tall,
fat book. He said it was a good harvest and that my ears must
be very fertile.

We've finished the trees and tomorrow we'll start on the fruit-
bearing plants. He tries to stay ahead of me by reading books
he's hidden. I overhear him whispering the Latin and English
names in the TV room.

But it's the Indian names that quiet him. He says the most
peculiar thing after I tell him the secret names of salal and the
story-trail they lead us to.

*You know what, Uncle? Everything I was thinking, except your
voice, went away when you were saying that story.*

Perfection of What No One Taught Him
for Chris

I.

I burned the crane feather I found
the day before and told my brother,
the gifted one, the cold would fall off him
as he walked the next day at dawn
and the weight would rise like smoke
out of his bones that night while he slept.
And he would sleep, I assured him.

We still shared a room and often woke
each other from nightmares,

or to watch the snow falling,
or the lightning, or to see a sunrise
stretched out over ribs of clouds,
or wind smacking the trees around,
or swift clouds letting out moonlight
in flashes—torn remnants of light.

The feather didn't belong in my hand
the way it fit my brother's.
The clarity I've often heard of
has never gathered in my mind
as it should after brushing someone's
troubles away with a feather
that always turns up just in time.

II.

From our bedroom window my brother
had watched, horribly rapt, a tiny wolf
being eaten by a rat: a frothy squealing
that woke him. And then a second rat,
the smallest of the three dark beings,
swallowed the other two in a single gulp.

Keeping its eyes on my brother
the remaining rat, there or not there,
backed away and grew smaller,
as though the few steps back
were each a yard long, until it vanished —
the full moon pulled its light in some.

And then my brother, sobbing.

III.

I never let on I knew why
Dad explained away the vision:
I'd overheard him telling Mom
that when he was eight he'd seen
two frogs eat a tiny black wolf
the day before his mother died.

What my brother saw or dreamed
was on the night before Grandpa died
and the night before I saw Mom weep,

looking as though she might vanish the way
the rat did. Already she seemed smaller.

It was dawn
and my brother was out walking
when the phone rang too early
to be carrying ordinary chat.

IV.

What was I dreaming
the last time
my brother woke me?

Dad was walking across
our dry fields, more than
halfway across, but no longer
getting any farther away.

Being Turned Back

I.

Before false dawn's heavy fall,
prayers all the way through in **SENĆOŦEN**.
I've never dreamed where they go—
rain carried past in clouds
that look like a fleet of ships,
stars like water skillfully disturbed,
simplifying what I know about
a cloud's momentum in the dark.
A song then refuses to stand up in me
to the beat of two small maple paddles
my brother made. But it's okay to carry
a knot of song into the hills
when learning how to live beyond
the voices that never want to come here,
would turn me away from any good path.

II.

Deer Mountain, the blue grouse live here now—
the flat before the marsh, their stirring in water
shallowed by the innards of spring. Even the air
will seem derived from this spring's fatty light.
When false dawn fades, it seems pushed
or pulled through the pores of a body
the sun completes. And then a third body
at the top of the short hill after the stretch
of trail full of throaty grouse quibble:
a buck in his prime, perhaps feeling
he's come home at last.

III.

When meeting an animal on its path, in its territory:
> Awake before sunrise. *Check.*
> Pray to all that names them. *Check.*
> Wait long enough to be sure
> the song for that morning
> actually wasn't ready to come. *Check.*
> Wait for the nagging voices to quiet. *Check.*
> Not to mention I may be the last
> to run here barefoot!

IV.

The buck lowers his head and shakes it as though to show me his antlers are well attached. When he lifts his head back up he grunts out a steamy snort. I don't look into his eyes, aware I must be human stench above all else; only ten feet away, I fear being seen as I am, or to insult his weak eyes by looking into them. Using his best **SENĆOŦEN** name I ask which way he's planning to run so I can stay out of the way. He answers by lowering his head and digging at the bare mountain under his feet. The clacks of his hooves seem to fall too lightly when he charges. I yell over my shoulder in gasps of **SENĆOŦEN**, "I don't understand! I don't understand! I'm carrying only my best intentions, cousin!"

He stops running after me and yells down, dumbfounded amusement shivering through his voice, something like—*but you're carrying tears in your pockets, or you've got sorrow in your hair: I don't want this in my hills!* His ancient dialect rolls a steam so sweet off his tongue. I hear the trees shamelessly leaning in to inhale some, wishing, as I have since, to be full of words to sing the same song the trees and the deer, or rather their grandfathers, surely sang to our first generation.

Waiting for the Sun

I ask uncle if he'd like help down the trail
to Grandma's beach, offering my arm.
He's not even fifty-five yet, but I'm thirty
and this is my only turn to hold the prod.
He sits on a stump to undress. (Don't tell him,
but I hope I'm young as he is when I'm his age.)
Thank you for Uncle, I imagine saying
to false dawn's mountain across the bay.
I joke to Uncle he shouldn't feel ashamed
if he needs help standing up from the stump.

Summer and we are waiting for the sun:
it's something he's teaching me.
He chuckles (I've got the prod — it's my turn)
Ohhhh boy, he laughs, *your time will come,
your time will come*. He exaggerates a nod,
looking down, then he turns his face back up
and his glance touches the mountain darkly
before he looks back to me, smiling.

The old sun finally drags its ass
over the east hills. *'Bout time*, Uncle says,
or the otter farther south along the beach says it.

Finished our wishes and thank you's, we turn
and walk weightlessly clumsy to shore.
On the shining flat of water at high ebb,
our wakes open like arms and dissolve.

I say over my shoulder, *Uncle, you let me know*
right way, now, if you feel any pains
in your chest, or arms, 'kay?

He laughs a little louder
to conjure made-up disgust
and sits down on his stump.
It's not lonely.

Through the Kitchen Window

After my brother Chris's poem of the same title

Messy tufts of grass,
the best for making the snake song,
hands pressed together
as if praying, or blowing harmonica.

Spear grass bent over, heads full of rain.
Some folded by the weight,
jointed where their stems collapsed.

I am staring much as my mother did
watching Dad in his garden, reading
his gestures—what he didn't share
about the narrowing passage
his days were becoming.

I learn only now
many of the grasses are not native—
it would have been a good joke
to share with a father like mine.

As it turns out, in those narrowing days
half his will walked astride
the season's trudge,
arranged our hours at home
to an ancient composure,
all the family gathered
around one piece of turned soil,
some idea we all believed about the world—

I don't know how.

Mom, up late canning the tomatoes,
and up early to make the morning pancakes
singing to the rhythm
she made turning the batter —
                    I don't know how.

I climb up on the counter
to open the little window.
Squeezing through and sliding
awkwardly headfirst, I become
my mother's gaze.

But what I wish for most
is for Dad to be in his garden,
despite what I've let it become
so we can share a joke, open
wider his path, narrowing
thought by thought: shrewder
competition for the light.

Building My Home in Your Mind

In the afternoon, after work, is the best napping time.
The best time for coffee and daydreams
is ridiculously early morning. The best time to make love
is when the high is going out. The best time for new snow
is at the dark end of the walk. When there is a fire waiting
is the best time to be miserable, wet up to your knees
after you hiked days into the trees. Tears are best held
when there are tears rightly put before your own,
best offered when you can faithfully recall
the one who used to hold you as the one who would
hold you through. Late spring is the best frog time.
The best trout time comes soon after.
When the harshest wind that drives through this town
drives through, that's when you'll remember
the smallness of your being. This is also the best time
to remember how afraid Aunty is of the wind
—and your love for her —*and* just how she wears that fear.

Your mother used to pray for planes sputtering overhead
during a storm, which has become the best time to remember
your mother's prayers, how you once imagined her voice
not dissolving, as sound does, but travelling beyond the cold
to where the sun was just rising for a humid day
and someone so plainly forgot to make their bed
for the first time so late in life. The best time to light
too many candles is when you wish for too many candles.
The best time to drink too much red wine is when you've forgotten
how sad it makes you and how the cruder machinery
of your hometown is slowly drowning out its original song.

The best time to lie down on the floor with your dog
is after getting drunk with the stupidest people you go on loving.

The best time to listen intently to a wind-blown rain is when
you are completely apathetic or too heart-tender, yet exhume visions
of your half-naked father in threadbare gumboots and thin underwear,
rattling blindly in the late and early-morning hours
to upturn a garbage can under your bedroom window,
knowing how much you love the sound of rain —
this is the best time to accept the apologies he never spoke.

II.

Wyoming, Too Much for Me

Love the distant mountain.
Love its shadows.
Love its gleaming ice cap,
it's low-down gleaming.
You'd start walking toward it,
if you didn't know better.
You start walking.

Released from an Ordinary Night

And then you hear a rabbit screaming.
How the frogs and crickets empty the night
all the way up to its feeble stars: end of summer.
Even the frogs and crickets, you imagine,
close their eyes. You close your eyes.

Something has the rabbit,
a young owl baffled by what it's done.

You turn away as you would from
someone dumbly staring at you
in a public place. Nothing stands upright
with the oaks and the underbrush but
the rabbit's squealing, its crude death.

You want anything else and go walking.
If only to find someone up late. You want talk,
or to stand again with frogs and crickets
singing their unassuming song.

At the bus stop, there's a man
you can tell is fresh out of jail.
What he expects is to be stood away from,
something he can't yet believe
will ever be different. Yet he hopes
there are instincts that return.
For now he's trying to remember
how to stand at a bus stop, where to look
when a stranger comes near.

About the screaming and abrupt silences
he could teach you. He knows
what will send someone looking
for dull conversation. He doesn't expect
you to go to him for salvation:

At the bus stop you offer him a hand.
He practises his handshake on you.

When Asking of a Man

The police officer who pulls me over
for walking at 5 A.M. says nothing
while he sobs and arranges me
against a dawn-coloured wall.

No answers in my socks.
None in my pockets, dry
white tongues choked-out.
No answers under my hat.

Done with me, he continues
frisking up the wall, until
it's the sky he suspects
of withholding—pockets
in the clouds of the sky?
Empty.

Back down the old wall
he stops, thumbing, as though
trying to turn back a page,
where the mortar is sloppy—
end of a day a half century ago,
the mason's apprentice
looked back when he heard
a girl approaching behind him.

Leaving me splayed against
dawn, he walks to the curb
and sits in one lamentful flop.

As if from Chinese dinner,
the night before, he unrolls
what he believes will be
his fortune. It says only: *No.*
He sobs "No," over and over
while the lights from his cruiser
flap across his shiny badge
and polished boots, the rumple
of him sitting there, his face wet,
his shirt untucked.

Cigarettes in a One-Pub Town

The pub closes and its people carry little torches.
The locals know the road so I follow the trailing-
off, the brightening and dimming, the little burning
they draw closer to their lips.

I am with the girl who soberly asked if
I was going home with her that night.
"You might," she explained, "end up in
the wrong hands otherwise."

On the Road of Little Torches,
she asks to hold my hand.

Three guys laugh and stumble
from one of the invisible paths. No torches.
The talker in their group asks for cigarettes.
"Only three left," she says,
but she will share one,
two of the guys can share one,
and she'll have one left for morning.
"Yeah, for morning!" one of them laughs.
I catch the joke and wonder where I'm going.

Hooting nearly all the way up to the dead end,
loud *Good nights* drilled into the hollowing dark,
only two torches remain on the road.
The three guys break off in the direction
of a house with one orange, burning window—
"So she never came back for that ugly orange dress…"

says *my girl*, a name I start calling her
to sturdy me inside the invisibilities
her town is made of. Reeling back toward
her guys — my name for them — she yells,
"The dress makes a better curtain anyway!"

"Oh, thanks for the cigarette, by the way,"
their quiet one shouts back. The end of his silence
somehow pleases me: "And oh. Nice to meet you...
Umm, well, lucky man anyway," the quiet one says.
The others grunt their agreement and then I'm part
of one of those loud *Good nights* when I shout back,
"Likewise, o' men of the orange-dressed-window!"

Lying with me, she smokes her last cigarette.
How I nearly burn down inside
the tender despair we become
the instant after I dress. Around her eyes,
the cigarette-bloom and wither.
And the point of fire in her pupils.

After she walks me to my campsite
I remember I am wearing a friend's coat,
and offer her the unopened pack of smokes
I find in the pocket. We stop on the severe edge
of light slapped down by streetlamps
at the gate: a tourist's doorway — dumb light.

But it is along the dark road to her place
the hitch of an unnamed thing
between her guys and her
made something fine out of the night
despite all that threatened
to make us terribly ordinary—

along the Road of Little Torches, cigarettes
passing hand to hand, mouth to mouth.

Elsewhere

There was a river with no name.

The bridge being built across
will always have a void between the two sides
because your stay in that strange
little town, at last you knew, was over.

You never told her where you were
before you met her in her town.
You also knew you spoke of it
every time she caught you staring off.

When she speaks in her sleep,
her voice is rich with the other dreaming:
This is not your home. You could
never live here. Go home.

Having Never Seen Fireflies

The restaurant's closing—tea lights
going out, up in the main room
and along the bar, and up
the stairs just behind. Some expand:
little flames giving a last kick
before they narrow and sink.
Some nearly go out
but come back a little smaller
like candles on a grave appear smaller
every time an urge turns you back.

A few times it has seemed to you
the sunlight was carrying rain in it
as it fell, or each drop of rain
was carrying light.

For all you know, fireflies could be biters,
landing like sparks on your naked legs,
rolling you out of the very spell they
lulled you into—humid night.

You were rocking
in the soft mouth of the waitress
who tongues you back
out of the way like gum
when she plainly asks,
peering over the dying
candles in her tray,
if there'll be anything else
or just the bill.

After Cutting Off My Right Arm

No one asks me anything, even
though I've painted on the front
and back of all my T-shirts, *ASK*.

Ask me why I walk as though
the darkening sky, messy clouds,
are sitting on my head.

Ask me why the dog and I
go out alone now, and often.

Ask me why I seem smaller
—as I must—sitting behind
the wheel of my car, leaving,
returning with nothing—
hours never asked about.

When I stop outside your little house
and raise my left arm to wave,
invite me in or ask why these days
I stand there a little longer—too long
to be someone just passing by.

Failing to Be Dreams

It seems to me as though I'd be saying to her
Here, hold this, then handing her smoke
or light or the shadow from a passing bird.

What are my plans, then?

It seems to me someone's just demanded
Here, hold this, and handed me ashes
in wind or ambers in rain—blindness.

I know the weight of my days
only through those who ask blandly
where I'm going—blindnesses.

Will I have children?

The shadows are heavying
though they are lighter
than the birds tearing through.

Ease of the Lonely Vision

I feel so weak tonight I could fall in love
with a crane-fly. Having never thought of myself
a typical male, I suppose, makes me a typical male:
their long legs, wispy way of going about things—

The one plucking madly at the window's rain-
strings; the one rocking to sleep in the room's air
moored by her front legs to the dusty ceiling;
the one falling from the sill's candle, gracefully.

In sucked-back tide of light at dusk,
one crane-fly heaves as if drowning,
a mockery of love and death, the way it shines—
it's the way its fragility is not encumbered by mine.

The Drunk Dog

Poor dog. Whiskey-hearted.
Fat froth around your mouth.

Sit. Give a paw.

Your body has become the eye
I can nearly see us through,
all of us falling or something.
Your body's become an ear
at the centre of human chinwag.

Sadly, what someone has made
absent in you, is being snuffed out
on the midnight highways.
And your chance to go home
is being buried by the slow creep
of houses up into your hills
with inventions of equally
drunken thoughtlessness.

Your condition and ours: one
a slopped-in impoverishment.
The other: tough poverty,
walking too self-consciously
upright to pass as sober
or well intentioned.

One hopeful apology stands
in a holy doorway it cannot enter.

Please,

lie down.

Soon you will fall
into a pitiful drunk man's sleep.

For the Poet's Lover

A poet: one who constantly thinks of something else;
his absent-mindedness drives his people to despair.

— Czeslaw Milosz

I love the rain and forgetting.
My attention will pack its one blue
suitcase and leave town,
without warning or regret,
when I feel the fevered need
to dance. Dance of the midnight
bed, dance at dawn along the thin
lines of tender seedlings—because
I've changed my mind about keeping
a garden this year. And the stomping
dance along the imagined path
pointed away and downhill
from the one thing, this time,
I know I want
to end.

I've loved the body
in a deathbed too many times.
Over breakfast or while watching
a movie from our sofa, I still
return to the deathbeds and the last
days of rude breathing.
There, a sad currency of words.
We whisper until we are broke.

At the edge of the hayfields
with you, I love the sad-looking deer
standing in the rain.

When we walk down
our street, holding hands,
I leave our story to remain
with the shy dog sleeping
in the mud in front of a house
with no curtains.

Your Lover Brings You

Your lover brings you
the skeleton of an oak leaf
as if she'd unhung a spiderweb
and carried it home.
She hauls into the bedroom
a long dirty branch to show you
the colours it's marked with,
made by other windfall piled across it.
She brings you a pheasant tail-feather
to show the bluish seedling
growing inside its stem. Imagine
the stone she brings you
stained with the shape
of a sleeping frog: tiny hibernation.
She rests it in a bird's nest
built entirely of your dog's fur—
the dog two years gone
into another sleeping.

And when she brings you a candle
the times your sleeplessness
terrifies you, through the opened window
you feel she has drawn close
the night's spherical breathing.

So when she brings you tears,
they're in a language
she has nearly prepared you for—
what else, but give, then,

what you habitually withhold,
so that offering it
is as exceptional
as her otherwise casual wonder:
words inside the smallest rooms,
too small for us to wholly enter.

Prayer to End Silences
For Michelle

I pray for you when getting it wrong in her poems
sends her walking into the belly of our street—
darkness that lingers late into the day.
If only you could see her sink into fog that closes
right behind her. What she carries
night and day for you—I don't know
what it is. I know her drowning in fog
with the night around her shoulders.

You have no name; she hasn't spoken it.
Smoke rolling out in curls
into a tangle above my smudge bowl
knows you. The staccato lines of my prayer
reach silence where your name should be.
Only the collapse of something
between my stomach and my lungs
confirms you namelessly. What rides up
in the braiding and unbraiding of smoke
is made of your daughter's losses—
wandering, leaned over a book,
walking across the lawn toward home
with her head down. The hours
she's sat up in bed while I invented
one breath after the other in the dark.
Your tears, her silence and mine: lesser prayer.

I call to my side those who will carry
my prayers to you and finally take up
the only name I have that they might find you by:

Take pity on "Dad," I whisper.
Put a blanket around Dad's shoulders.
Put grand torches along Dad's waning path.
Take pity on Dad that he might go
where proper tears can take him.

Gathering to Sing *The Laughing Song*

I grew up in a town peopled with those
I'd once hated. Now I'm too tired to hate
those whose hunger drives them mad.

I haven't moved. I haven't even changed
my phone number. And some still call
looking for Mom and Dad. I say to the phone
I'm sorry, though I don't feel sorry.
Often the caller is someone who knew me
before my remembering started. I repeat
the month and year of each parent's death
as though giving a new address.

As I grew up, it became harder to tell stories
about the people I loved, gathering
along the lines of my revisions of them.
But then those I grew up with started reappearing:
from prison, divorces, addictions, near-death
epiphanies; all simple grown-ups carrying on.

One had learned what killing someone was—
the death he brought, a heaven compared
to being the body inside which
conscience stands and sits and lies
down with rigid non-compliance.

One knew what it looked like
when a police officer, disarmed, shot in the knee
broke down well beyond ordinary humanness,

into "hilarious" caged-dog whining:
the way all police seem to him now.

Finally, the one you could say I loved best,
drove whatever, wherever without looking back
or looking in. It was meaty-naked paranoia
that sent him into blabbering confession,
to the station and then three years in maximum.

None of the first loves returned.
One murdered, one better off dead,
one lost and often asked after.

When I grew up I wasn't doing
what my dreaming promised a far-off self
I'd be doing. What I'd learned best
was only to withhold what others
would have me give. And having
walked away from so many things
I was now running into what
I'd walked from already,
more than once.

A Giving to the Dispossessed

Put off by the racket at the pub, I crouch outside,
lean against a brick building. When I close my eyes,
a man's voice starts singing to a beat he makes
                slapping the surface of water.

When I open my eyes his singing ends abruptly
as it started. I spring to my feet and check around
for anyone who might be watching. I close my eyes again
for two beats of song. I breathe —
                walk two or three miles of silence.

In the gritty echoing of my footsteps
the voice speaks in the language I come from.
Eyes opened, closed, opened again,
standing in the dumb orange of a streetlight.

The voice says,   *It was a long and cumbersome*
                    journey to find you.

A few notes of song.

                    But every step closer
                    assured me this would
                    not be a wasted effort.

Song slapped to water again.

                    What work we have.
                    What remembering.

Late Summer Rain

Night's marked now.
In the ear, rain scratches down
the entire height of the dark.

Fat sockeye are ready
to go home and die.
After that, nothing stops
the way it did
for summer.

The night shivers
anywhere the rain touches it,
as though it wasn't expecting
such a hard falling. Those
listening put on their surprise
despite the cooler days,
and the sun's late rising.

The last brittle oak leaves,
shredded down to their bones,
sound the rain's softness,
while a scout wind rides
steady over the treetops.

The wind sounds
as though it's dragging something
long and ragged
behind it.

Making the Forgotten

Tail feather from a bald eagle.
I carried it from the north islands
to her new city so she could
hang it over her bed.

Returned to me in the mail
in the same wooden box
I made for it. I drove for hours,
wondering what really carries us
to the absolute wreck of something
until we can drive away.

I gave the feather to a river.
If it sang, falling from the bridge,
the river sang louder.

III.

I'll Be Done This Soon

I don't feel the urge
to excuse myself.
In the crossfire
of others' plans for me,
I found my loneliness
was made of this.

To keep the last
smouldering punk going,
I cried until I could hear
my own wish-filled voice.
It was dispossessed of
the other pieces of a whole,
or cast aside by a summer dream
in the slope, now wintering.
It was even below the gushing
run-off and crying wind.

Finally, I said, and took off
my shoes. Down there,
no shelter I build for myself
or anyone might build for me
could ever last.

Pathway

Walking on your heals
down the hill
after a seven-day fast,
your thoughts are thrown about
by the sound of two streams
you are walking between.

Nothing seems your own.
Your weakened body
belongs to the earth,
your feet being tossed
downhill. Your thoughts go
where they want to,
or enter from dawn's push
upstream. Where the water
gives itself in rolling heaves
and hushed strands
under the willows.

When one stream runs harder
than the other, you feel
you are walking close
to a shivering wall
with something at its foot
being smoothly born —
the other stream.
Your solitary instruction
enters where both streams
are calm: *Start walking.*

You are alone now.
How is the quiet teaching you?

We don't even get
to take our faces with us,
when our short visit here
ends, while speaking
of you has always
meant a quick vision
of mostly your face —
touched gently once
by the back of a woman's hand,
but never again by that woman.

Your thoughts would not stop
going to her. How is memory
teaching you? One family
calls the north stream
Tangled Rope, and
the south *Looking Ahead*.
One family calls the north
Hand Over Hand
and the south *Enters
Second*. Your family calls
them, simply, *The One on
This Side* and *The One on
That Side*. Your favourite
cousin found that amusing.

When you were both
still young enough to play
while everyone else worked,
the two of you, standing
one behind the other,
jumped together, a half-turn
one way then a half-turn back
singing, *The one on this side
and the one on that side!*

You sang and danced
until you collapsed
from laughter-exhaustion.
His family had no names
for the two streams yet.
His father being from elsewhere,
he was still silenced
walking everywhere
with his wife's brother:
watching raises the sound
of your own breathing—
the breath teaches you.

More than halfway down,
a thought invades:
depending on the spot
you chose, if you dug
a small channel between

the two streams, one stream
would become weaker.
This is the face of something.
It will keep its face
through each renewal
of your family. This is how
hunger teaches — by wrapping
the one true longing around
your shoulders. Your family
will be as it is, only once.
Another face.
With darkness for a skull?

Nearly down to the hard silt
where the streams join
to make a tough estuary,
you realize you haven't
once looked up. Left at
the foot of the hill
by your grandfather,
now it's your father riding
the full glare of morning
in a small canoe.
You will both arrive
at the same time
at the *Dirty Nose*
(everybody calls
the hard silt that).

You won't learn anything
from this impossible timing
for many years.

When you climb aboard
the canoe, your relief
wordlessly tells you
what you learned
in the hills, something
you won't mention
for at least a year.

You've been shown
the long, casual stride
of seasons. Each season
is much taller than all
the pungent wild land
that owns you.
Each season walking
with its head tipped
slightly up, as if dreaming,
You will never see their faces.

A Whale Can Bring You to Where It Starts

The kayaks are moored
and now you have a try at believing
something dumbfounding-enormous
rose earlier in day,
just for a breath,
looked at you and understood you were there.

The wet eye stayed on you
while the whale rolled away,
then the wet eye closed as the whale sunk
in surrender to its weight inside water.
The water's surface hunched up
then caved in.

Its solitude meant its age.
Its curiosity meant its age.
Its staggered route meant it was
staying near the warmer currents.
The well-healed tear in its tail meant
as a calf swimming shallow
it was driven over by a motorboat.

But what of its soft wet eye closing
as the whale rolled away and sank?

Sweeping the Pool

Rainwater from two mountains
gathers here and throws its weight
around. After tasting the fresh water
at the edge of the estuary, salmon run
in just so far, then back out to where
the other unturned salmon gather.
The water's taller than me, but I know
where to stand. Dad and my uncles
arranged a proper introduction:

Lesser Stream, this is Kevin.
Don't eat him.

So I'm chest-deep in swift water,
toeing around an edge I've never seen.
Please don't eat me.

I shoulder my long-handled dip net
like a flag: *best aluminum,*
corrosion-resistant mesh
and water-resistant grip.

A white man yells at me from across
the stream: "If you people are going to fish
in your traditional fishing grounds,
you should use traditional fishing gear!"

I ignore him but he keeps yelling
in bigger vowels, louder each time.

He looks around seventy, so I shout
back in my language and then his,
saying nearly the same thing in both:
"Mind your manners or I'll eat *you!*"

He flaps both hands at me then stomps
away, puppet to a bad puppeteer.

The pool is about the length of a grave.
How do I know? I've grown into habit
for this place: the pool and the edge,
stirring my reflection every time
I turn a new face down into the dark water.
Where I dig my net I do so carefully,
so it doesn't get so heavy I can't pull it up.
So it doesn't get so heavy,
it pulls my ear to its hard secrets.

Please Come Back When My House Is Warmer

Young's "icy sky at night" strikes you
as a little dull this evening–
babies' wet mouths as they tip away from the breast
and their clear, blind eyes going out.

There were parts of the journey you couldn't see
in the days before your conception,
yet even then voices called back with a strain in them:
May you not be born, as winter babies so often are,
with the kinds of wishes that grow heavier each year.
I hope for you early wisdom to spare you
from perceived expectations. You go back to bed.
Your curtains are raggy, the dog starts digging
at your shoulder to wake you. The hungry gold fish
and stinking fridge enter your half-conscious dreaming.
Near midnight, you watch the dog fevered-happy
out in the snow, and long stands of heavy cloud
sliding across the stars, some breaking into two or three pieces
before they're lost in the mess covering the sky.
And then there is only one star seeming undefeated.
Where it is fixed, you can still see the staggering traffic
of clouds moving on, and two memories strike you.

First, those you witnessed or read about who worked
a full life toward peace and found death a disappointing end.
Then, the room you entered to arrive here; the poverty
and helplessness of the people you were leaving to join
came in faces casting up their dying eyes. And there was a doubt.
You spoke to the room, *I'm sorry, I may not be as I'd hoped*—

one of those who can help you, and looked back
at the only door in the room, half open, light shivering through
as though on the other side of it you'd been sitting around a fire
where probably someone was still waiting tearfully for you.

The Man in My Ear's Light

I.

From early memory: you were left alone
with an old Dutch jeweller. Or were you?
It seems as likely as it does unlikely
you were left alone with a stranger back then.
But with a white man? The jeweller
was nearly deaf so he talked a lot
to entertain you, or to avoid the listening
that embarrassed him. You remember
an odd and alluring window he stood at.
While he talked, he squinted at gem after gem
held up to the setting sun.

I mean, if he even existed.

II.

As if clamping the tweezers on a rare gem
and holding it up in sunlight to measure it
flaw by flaw. Not considering a gem as rare
and flawless might suspend the same light dully.
Not considering the gem's flaws
as the old hunters knew each wolf from another
by their distinct markings.
The man leading the men's hunt
would put a corn seed down
in a paw print in the snow.
This was done to wish the wolves
a successful hunt and to honour

an otherwise-forgotten union.
Not considering the amber sapphire
that travelled to the New World for an impeccable cut,
may offer less than the rats' eyes gleaming
in the unharvested pumpkin field,
as headlights swung and the drivers drove.
October slows everything in its fog.
Consider how the rats' eyes make one mind
that sends a shiver and one mind that
vaguely challenges the crude gauge.
Consider two rats playing in headlights.
Someone parked at the field's edge,
and the rats running in mad circles
as your dog used to after a bath,
as you did as a child laughing deliriously,
unembarrassed by laughing
just from running around and around.

III.

An orange streetlamp in a square gravel parking lot.
At the margin of the light, a poplar, the weed of trees.
When a wind splashes the salty gravel up into the poplar's flinch.
When the tree rocks stiffly, its leaves waver an erratic shining:
one hundred dancers shaking silver fans to the drum
of a candlelit rite, or a fire collapsing and a swarm of sparks
twirling up and drilling through into another place.

IV.

He holds the black mug loosely with both hands,
but doesn't lift it anymore because it's been empty
long enough that he's forgotten the habit.
The table's made of dark wood and behind him
a dark bough, a tree left heavy just so.
The bough shivers with small birds
in its few warm hours during day.
The day's dry heat was tamped out
as night shut wholly. Thirsty land that night.
Ambitious day, heavy with light;
ugly light from the kitchen window,
and his dark setting, make him paler.
You've put your head down
as if listening intently, but inside
you're sounding your special call: *I know,*
I know, I know. A single frog sounds only once
from across the yard, in Saanich
the call to vulnerability. You've been called
to consider why the world has sat you down
across the table from someone stressing the verses
of what you've heard many times before.

V.

You close your eyes.
The poplar living on the fringe of light
and the salty gravel make a brief display of fire;
that hill rattling with a candlelit rite.

Two rats climbing round and round
a cherry tree in the full light of the moon;
a new height it is raised to,
which you go on celebrating from then.
If you could go back again *this* year
to the unharvested pumpkin fields,
if you could go back and travel
with the old hunters, or the wolves.
If you could go back and run
in dumb circles and laugh.
If only you could remember what
the old Dutchman was telling you
about gems and sunlight.

VI.

What a Saanich Man owes, tonight, to a white man
marks you and marks all the withholding
of manhood from yourself. The kitchen light is off.
Only one messy candle and a dark cloud's ragged moon
offer light: one is offering up, the other is offering down.
You tip your head up and your thoughts gather.
He nearly smiles—then continues the hard drive through
a young and hefty deafness, perhaps sensing you've finally
conceived of all the long years that made him,
promises only time can keep. Perhaps he senses
you've finally placed your story in reach of his.

Whatever carries the light in your ears, leads his words in.

Perching

On the dock, an old Chinese man
eats bait-fish raw. "Beautiful, *beautiful*.
Anything what live under water.
What beautiful!"

Where a narrow plank replaced
one nearly twice as broad
I lay down my left eyebrow, left eye
to see what the aging wharf usually hides:

in the darkness, thin bars of sunlight
on the water and gas-swirl that passed
by like a slow run of colourful flames,
reflection of my eye in a prison burning
down. Deeper, perch were playing
and some resting, going nowhere.
The ones playing looked like leaves
in a breeze — now and then I got the glare
of their gold and silver sides.

The one he held up twitched,
part of its brain still dreaming
of the weightlessness and dark.
"What name for these?"
"Perch."
"No, no, what *name*?"

Whechie, I say just as he said *beautiful*.
Whechie, just as my dad used to say it.

If You Remember the Names of the Winds

After my grandfather's unfinished autobiography

Two winds touch. They have already
stepped back from their embrace
when those who know how they long
for each other turn; knowing, too,
how seldom they visit, brings
an occasion few are left to share.

From the few words the two winds need
to exchange, a snow whirls, breaking
the tense rising of the spring.
JÁN ÍY ȻENs NE̱NET ĆELĆELA̱NEN
an old man blabbers drunkenly up
from a park bench: an awakening
flatly dismissed by passersby.

Not quite three blocks away,
looking up from his studies, a young man
translates by speaking the one language
he knows: *Welcome home Ancient Ones,*
meaning also he understands their pain
is a sweetness some drop all other chores
to go inward in search of.

Brentwood Bay

The *town* of Brentwood Bay—
not my home, but surrounded
by the entire mathematics
of postal codes that add up
to my "home site."

Yet somehow a fitting part
of Saanich in all my dreams
of Saanich: a grave marker?
No, the town wasn't made
to keep our remembering
and forgetting.

East end: filled-in bog.
Cranberries and medicine,
only women were invited there.
Its burial answered to
by my great-grandma's tears—
the only answer.

West end: our winter
sanctuary—winter jack-springs,
crabs, oh, clams and blue
grouse. In one hour of night,
a celebration's worth of grouse
could be gathered from low branches
of young pines. My mind
sometimes gropes in the dark
for their scaly ankles.

South: more bog, and deer.

North: I live here,
A forest as my backyard,
a town out front.

I make another explanation
to myself: one built of tears,
the other entered,
piece by piece,
as best and sooner
than I could accept it.

Answering an Urge

Sun blazing early. Trail to the beach
not yet bothered, so I walk awkwardly,
forward and backward the same
number of strides, maybe to clear
the path for those who come next
with the same idea—that our childhoods
are still splashing around down here.

A waft of wind rolls up the hill
carrying the smell of juniper and ocean.
The bushy heads of spear grass heavy
with dew, and piss from wild packs of dogs
not yet evaporated, not even steaming.
On both sides of the trail the spear grass seem shy,
faces slightly turned-down, teetering
as the shy do one foot to the other,
but in that steady roll of wind.

Bare feet burrowed into the warm sand,
the slow, slopping waves draw me in
as a fire will net your attention into a lost-
like stare. The heat sweats out
a biting scent from the juniper
and a change of wind drapes the scent
around my shoulders.

Feeling so fine, I silently recite the names—
those who will never come here again.
The waves slide farther out
and my long list turns around on itself.

Maybe you have to walk in an uncolonized field
and have a thin vine draw its thorny body
across your ankle. This vine is what
Saanich people mean when they speak
of blackberries—the invisible mist at dusk,
air saturated with the odour of wild grasses
and the occasional whiff of ocean-side juniper,
the stinging scratch and slight weeping of my blood:
the wild meadow's own recipe for the air
from which the Saanich desire grows.

Baby

For Malcolm

If I hadn't already grown
into time and place, my name
would be waiting. When it is time,
whether by fire or decay, for me
to go, my name will live in
the hills. The hills will keep me
a secret until it's time again.

NI. NI QENNET TₜE W̲,SÁNEĆ —
Look. Look what's emerging,
the eldest of his time said, after
the flood was over. And, helped down
from the canoe by a young man at his elbow,
the old man explained, *What I mean by "emerging"*
is this baby. By the long labour of days
he'd witnessed the shape emerge from the water—
a baby sleeping on its belly with its bottom raised
up. That old man's name has long been secret
now. Those who know his name know he left
one kneeprint, a print from each hand
and tears in the mud where they landed home.
He said, *Baby*, and threw his name into the hills,
as long as this place will hold me, and I am
privileged to call this home, I will be baby.

The Laughing Face of Impermanence

In response to Kroetsch's absences in Seed Catalogue

Growing in the very hills
from where our language was barrowed

the presence of arbutus,
        the great-great-grandchild,
        the tree planted by a Saanich man
        whose name is in these hills

the presence of barefoot children
        told language enters
        through the feet

the presence of a pathway
        named for the beginning of a family
        and the horror of their disappearance

the presence of ȻOLOWENȾEȽ,
        another name yet to be carried down
        from these hills;
        too heavy still, that name

the presence of great healers
        whose lives are evermore private

the presence of dancers whose lives
        are more and more intruded upon

the presence of winds, whose names
        came up through someone's feet,
        and arrive precisely when we need them
        or right on time, at least

the presence of streams named
        by the sound they make
        in the Saanich ear,
        WEĆEĆE, for instance
        water falling on hard sand

the presence of streams named
        to remind us of our role in the wild —
        ḴENNES —
        meaning whale, meaning the body
        that returned to the sea,
        meaning the stream is calling
        though the lover cannot return

the presence of steams named
        for sleeping in late: **SELEKTEⱢ**,
        meaning the lesser stream, meaning
        it's smaller than the one beside it
        meaning if you slept in,
        that's where you'd be sent
        by your elders to fish, impossibly.

Here, borrow all that is still present:
you're walking all over it
and my people are dying.

And should you give it back
to where it laboured its first rising:
someone barefoot in these hills
will bleed from the mouth a word,
yet go on denying.

Singing Out the Fire

Looking out at me, old friend,
you must see a man too old
and too far along the trail
to travel home tonight.
But it is not yet so late
in all dreaming, not so late
in the very life of dreaming.
Still, I can't stay
with you much longer.

Grandpa told me—and I am
a grandfather myself now—
a man builds only one fire
in his lifetime, a fire he will bring
again and again. Old friend,
how much more willingly
you rise now—yet how hard
I wish, I can't stay with
you much longer.

While you tell me again
the story of our lifelong hunger,
fine beads of light
roll out on your breath:
something that you always take
back with you to the other world,
Grandpa told me.
I am the thankful student

who tended to your first sputtering
bloom into flames. I can't stay

with you much longer. My children,
each can bring their own fire
to turn to now. And they will be
ready to call you after I'm gone.
Maybe they will say,
Look. It's a fire like no other.